Published by Ad Hoc Fiction.
www.AdHocFiction.com

Purchasing Information:
Paperback available from www.AdHocFiction.com
E-book available from all usual outlets.

Printed in the United Kingdom.
First Printing 2021.

ISBN paperback 978-1-912095-45-2
ISBN e-Book 978-1-912095-44-5

Inside Fictional Minds

Tips from Psychology for Creating Characters

by

Dr Stephanie Carty

Contents

Introduction

You're going to need pockets and a shovel during our time together. The pockets should be deep enough to drop elements of learning into. As you go about your day, those ideas will jumble and tumble into place. The shovel is for digging below the surface, layer after layer.

Welcome to my brief guide to using psychological concepts to help form fictional characters with depth who interact and grow in ways that will resonate for readers.

The book is formed of short chapters as an easy first step to developing new ways of looking at your invented people. The topics have evolved from questions asked during my training courses with writers on the psychology of character. You will find recommended reading at the back of the book if you wish to delve further into any aspects. I've chosen to use 'they' when talking about your specific character in the singular rather than hop between he and she.

This book focuses on the everyday workings of characters rather than diagnoses or serial killers. What is it that makes people tick, what pushes them to act or avoid, why is one so different to another, and how can you show your character's unique internal world so it seems believable?

The first section will cover a wide range of topics about how characters (well, humans… but let's keep saying characters) feel, think and interact. The middle section will focus on specifics such as characters who have been through trauma or have perfectionist tendencies. The final section will focus on how you pull all the learning together in your writing project.

Whatever your genre, setting or audience, there are universal ideas that you can apply to suit your needs. They should be relevant to short stories, novels and plays. I will use the term 'story' throughout to cover all lengths.

Many of the topics overlap and are different approaches to exploring the same thing, so use whichever tasks seem helpful.

How to use the book

The ideas presented here can be used at the planning stage of your story, with characters in progress or during editing. I'd suggest you focus on one character at first across all the tasks to help you see how the ideas fit. However, if others shout for attention in certain sections, let them speak!

There are tasks attached to each topic. These should help you to personalise and solidify your learning.

The joy of fiction is that if you realise while working through the tasks that elements of your character don't add up or are not accounted for, you get to invent new behaviours or backstory.

However, I'm wary of being like my beloved childhood dictionary of dreams which professed to know exactly what an image or event in the dream-world meant as if that were universal. Hold the ideas I present as gently as a butterfly in the palm of your hand – clinging on too tightly may destroy any value in them to be adaptable for you and your characters.

As you read certain topics, it may be that your mind does what minds do, which is to draw associations between things. Before you know it, you may find that you're reflecting on your own history, beliefs, hidden longings and so on. This book focuses on characters but then we are all characters in our own and others' stories aren't we? Treat yourself kindly. This links us all. There's nothing wrong or broken about us, we are just busy being human.

What will psychological ideas add?

You don't need to write a single line about your character's childhood, beliefs, longings, or unconscious drivers in your story because they will play out through their actions and reactions. When you're clear about these it will colour not only what your characters say and do in the story but how you write scenes.

Your story doesn't have to focus on dramatic issues to benefit from psychological depth in your characters. Layered, believable characters lift any style of book because ultimately we want to create an emotional response. Whether we make readers laugh, cry, shake or gasp, psychologically informed writing is more likely to reach out and resonate. I get frustrated at a 'twist' that doesn't fit any of the evidence beforehand in the character and I feel nothing for a character going through hard times if it seems like I don't know them at all. That is not the same as making characters likeable. Readers don't need to like a character to be intrigued or invested in them.

Imagine I am your writing psychologist. This might be our conversation when discussing your character:

You tell me something your character does / hates / avoids / says.
I ask you WHY.

You give me an answer.
I say hmm, but what lies underneath that.

You answer.
I say ahh yes, but what lies underneath THAT?!

You get a bit irritated with me but then five minutes or five days or five weeks later, an answer forms that says more about the situation than you realised at the time.

I'll give you some examples as we progress so you can see this in action. Whatever your character is pulled to doing that is a problem for them in the story, there are likely to be layers of 'why' underneath.

Why are they drawn to 'bad' relationships, why do they say yes when they mean no, why do they pretend they're okay when they're struggling, why do they hurt people that they care about?

There's the in-the-moment 'why' that you may have made clear in the story. But there's probably also a whole history of how that pattern was formed and reinforced over time for your character.

The excavating that might seem unnecessary at first can unearth real gems way below the surface. Trust your gut. You've probably already planned or written layered aspects of your character without realising why you made the choices you did. Every day since childhood you've been absorbing the complexity of people, figuring future characters out by observing your own mind and making guesses about other people's.

Now make a start and see where the ideas and tasks take you. You can do them in order, at random, or pick what appeals. Do all the tasks to please the teacher-part of your mind or select one or two that you think fit with your own questions about your character. And remember, your unconscious mind works hard while you're doing something else entirely, so take breaks and be prepared for those elements to all come together in your deep pockets when you least expect it.

Part 1: The Basics

Overview of Emotions

Let's start with the basics of your character's emotional world. We all know what emotions are, right? Next time you're in conversation with someone, pay attention to what they say in sentences that start 'I feel...'. You may find that what follows isn't a feeling at all. In natural speech we often mix things up. 'I feel like a failure, I feel blocked, I feel fine, I feel like that wouldn't work.' It's not unusual for people to struggle to differentiate between emotions or confuse an emotion (e.g. anger) with a behaviour (aggression).

To strip it back to basics, it's helpful to think about what emotions a very young child is capable of experiencing. These can be considered our core emotional states that are in-built. Babies don't have the capacity to think about how they OUGHT to behave or feel so it's all on show, naturally flowing from one emotional state to another.

Although researchers vary slightly in what they deem to be the 'basic' emotions, the following list will give you a good starting point. Basic emotions can all be experienced by a young child (disgust is 'distaste' in babies at certain foods, then develops into more generalised disgust around age four).

Their expression is universally recognised. Basic emotions are produced automatically but the mind may quickly act to squash them down as we will discuss later.

Joy
Fear
Sadness
Anger
Surprise
Disgust

The 'complex' emotions are those which combine two or more basic emotions. The complex emotions have greater variability in how they appear than the basic emotions. Consider the ways in which personal and societal beliefs, expectations and values may influence them. You may need to think more carefully about how complex emotions are created, experienced and demonstrated by your character. They will be impacted by the era, location, societal rules, and so on that your story is set in. The complex emotions include:

Grief
Jealousy
Regret
Embarrassment
Guilt
Hate

Task 1

*Pick one complex emotion that your character experiences. Try to work out what combination of basic emotions go into the 'cocktail'.
(e.g. hate could be a combination of anger, fear and disgust)

*If you had to choose a maximum of three, what are the main basic and complex emotions that your character experiences along the journey of the story?

*Could a reader label these specific emotions in your character accurately without them being named in the story? You may want to ask a beta reader to see if they come up with something different!

Anger

Anger is a basic emotion that flares up before we can apply any kind of logic such as whether something was done to us by accident or on purpose. A part of the nervous system is triggered that causes physiological changes such as increased heart rate, raised blood pressure and an adrenaline boost. This response creates a surge of energy. The internal changes are automatic and involuntary.

'Healthy anger' has a key role in cueing us to set appropriate boundaries when others don't treat us well. Characters who really struggle to allow and acknowledge healthy anger will be more at risk of mistreatment due to poor boundary-setting. We will look more at this pattern in a later chapter.

Task 2

*Imagine you are reading a scene in a book in which a character is angry. What descriptions would you expect to see in terms of voice, body, movement, any other visible change?

*Think about the last time you felt angry with your parent, young child or boss. Write down what happened with your body language, voice, movement and any other obvious change?

*I think you can see where I'm going here. Compare the two lists. Any differences? If so, why?

We learn from a young age what emotions are 'acceptable' for us to have and in what situations. This learning can be from observing others, from being told off directly, or from more subtle cues like praise for masking an emotion. There are also influences wider than parenting like peers, teachers, the media, what's said in public spaces or what we see people 'like us' do on TV shows. Each of your characters will have had different messages about the acceptability of anger, as well as linked behaviours such as aggression or assertiveness.

It's not a case of simply copying parent behaviour. If your character had a violent parent, they may mirror some of what they experienced. However, they could work very hard to never be like their parent. This could be so extreme that they become fearful of even the HEALTHY version of anger, as their mind inaccurately links all anger to aggression. In this way, rather than becoming a bully, they may put themselves at greater risk of future maltreatment because they don't assert themselves when they are treated poorly by others.

Task 3

*What has your character learnt about the acceptability of feeling angry?

*Are there circumstances where it is deemed okay for them to feel anger?

*When, where and with whom is it deemed not okay?

There is a 'choice point' that happens between feeling the emotion of anger and choosing a behaviour. However, for characters with poor emotional regulation, it may seem there is no choice and they act before they can think. Poor self-regulation is more likely in those characters who never had a chance to learn how to self-soothe by being soothed by a caregiver as an infant. Certain substances, alcohol, sleep deprivation and physical pain can also make it harder to apply 'brakes' to behaviour.

Task 4

*How well can your character control their behaviour and make choices about how to act once they are angry?

*If it is hard for them to control their anger, have you considered:

a) their early experiences and ways in which they weren't helped to learn to self-soothe or self-regulate

b) other influences on poor control like alcohol or pain?

If your character is 'not permitted' to be angry, then what? They may work hard to hide their anger from others such as trying to control their body language and voice or avoid potential triggers. Or perhaps it is so deep-seated they hide the anger from THEMSELVES. As soon as anger is triggered, their unconscious mind may shut it down in different ways or turn it into looking like something completely different.

Here are some examples:

Anger turned into weepiness
Character A's father says something critical to her new partner. While trying to be assertive and discuss this, she finds herself weepy to the point that she can't tell her father he has been unfair and he should apologise.

Anger turned into numbness / dissociation
Character B has been shoved and ridiculed as he walks through a nightclub. He feels as if he's not really there and continues walking on automatic pilot.

Anger turned towards the self
Character C has had no sleep due to her baby crying. She is about to return to bed exhausted when her husband gets up for work noisily and wakes the baby. She tells herself she's a stupid, useless mother who doesn't deserve sleep while he works so hard to put food on the table.

Task 5

*Look for examples in your story where your character is or could be angry. Check whether their responses fit with their learning about anger as answered in the previous task.

*If there are circumstances where anger is NOT permissible in your character's mind, what could it turn into instead?

*Is this a deliberate choice by the character or an unconscious defence mechanism such as in the examples?

Anxiety

When you think about your character's anxiety, you may focus on their physical state of tension and associated body changes, or their internal world of worry, dread and inventing terrible future scenarios. Anxiety is an umbrella term for many different experiences. It is an important alert system to help keep us safe and motivated (and I guarantee you WILL recognise some of these symptoms in yourself at times). However, it can become excessive and disabling.

Let's start by thinking about the order in which changes happen in the body when someone experiences anxiety. This will help you determine where on the scale your character's physical symptoms fit for a specific scene. Anxiety shows itself in the body initially through muscle tension, which can build up into an over-aroused system. If anxiety isn't dealt with at this point, it can change into an under-aroused system.

1. *Muscle tension*
This starts in the hands, rises up the arms, the shoulders move upwards, then the face tenses with a furrowed brow and clenched teeth, then tension moves down to the torso such as holding the stomach in, down via clenched buttocks into the legs, ending with tense feet that may cross over each other or be raised up onto tiptoes while sitting.

2. *Over-arousal*
Examples of over-arousal include a surge of energy, faster breathing and heart rate, sweating, unable to keep still, dry mouth, urge to go to the toilet, racing mind.

3. *Under-arousal*
Anxiety that is not halted can cause a 'crash' down into a 'switched off' state. This can show itself in dizziness, confusion, ringing ears, blurred vision, nausea or diarrhoea, difficulty with speech or thinking, finding it hard to follow what is said, feeling numb or unreal.

As anxiety goes up and down, the symptoms change in severity and presentation.

You may be familiar with the over-arousal stage, also called 'fight or flight'. You will see how it mirrors the physical impact of stress or anger. Some characters will naturally channel this energy to escape, whereas others may act out with aggression or turn to panic. There may be times when the surge in energy means that your character can act quickly and effectively to do something really important, so the high arousal stage can sometimes be helpful.

The third stage is less recognised. It no longer looks like a nervous, shaking character whose mouth is too dry to speak. At this point, the mind goes into a form of 'shut down'. Rather than displaying tense muscles, the character would look floppy, day-dreaming or as if not interested. They may find it hard to concentrate or explain themselves well. Rather than feeling panicked, they may now experience a kind of numbness or dissociation (where the environment or the self seems unreal or dream-like).

If your character has experienced stress or anxiety for a long time then the above symptoms may well take their toll. For example, if muscles are constantly tensed that can cause chronic pain. Some of these body changes can become habitual, even when the character is NOT anxious. Your character may habitually use shallow breathing or have constant high muscle tension that feels 'normal' to them.

Now let's look at what's going on inside an anxious character's mind.

Anxiety lives off creating imagined futures. These can play out in detail and bring on the physical symptoms above even though none of what is feared has actually occurred. This is both the power and the curse of a human brain! The ability to leap ahead and create different versions of what could happen may be life-saving or life-draining for your character.

Anxious thoughts can come without your character choosing them – a kind of internal nagging voice about worst case scenarios. These thoughts may race from one awful thing to another or be stuck on a loop of the same worry.

Remember that most of the time while feeling anxious, your character will be in a 'high alert' state. If you're writing a scene in which they are anxious, check what their focus is (or if in third person, what the scene focus is, more on that later).

Having anxious thoughts and bodily symptoms is not the same as having an anxiety disorder, by the way.

Finally, there's how anxiety impacts your character's behaviour.

A common behaviour in the face of anxiety is to avoid whatever seems to bring on the physical and emotional sensations described above. Your character may do their best to avoid thoughts, feelings, people, places, and activities as a way to avoid the anxiety. This brings about a short-term relief. That relief then makes it more likely they avoid those things again in the future.

Task 6

*If there are sections of your story where your character is anxious, check to see if you have / can add body changes to match the level of anxiety appropriately.

*How have you / could you show what an anxious, hypervigilant mind would notice in specific scenes (e.g. where the exits are in a room)?

*Are you clear about what your character tends to do in response to anxiety?

Do they ignore and plough on, perhaps to the point of 'shutdown'?

Do they use avoidance to find relief?

Or do they have ways to reduce the physical signs (e.g. slow their breathing), thinking traps (e.g. talk themselves down or use self-soothing strategies) or do they not let anxious thoughts rule their behaviour (e.g. 'feel the fear and do it anyway')?

Loss

Loss may affect your character in many ways. It doesn't always mean losing a loved person to death.

Some other examples of where loss can occur:

- meaningful objects or places (e.g. forced to leave a home)
- social (e.g. pushed out of a friendship group)
- internal (e.g. loss of self-confidence)
- physical (e.g. chronic illness)

Some losses are temporary, others are permanent.

Grief is a natural response to loss. It is an intense emotional pain and sadness alongside yearning for who or what is no longer there.

If your character faces significant loss, it can be helpful to consider their personal journey of grief as being linked to numerous factors as in the following task.

Task 7

If your character experiences a significant loss within or before your story, consider whether any of the following would impact on how they deal with it:

Beliefs

Expectations

Relationship history

How much they allow help or comfort from others

Role they tend to take in the family / in social network

How much they usually focus on their internal world of thoughts and feelings

How much they tend to try to avoid painful emotions

How unexpected versus expected the loss was

What else was going on in their life

What they tend to prioritise

How central the loss is to the sense of self is useful to consider. Has the loss directly impacted your character's core identity such as seeing themselves mainly as a professional, a spouse or someone who helps anyone at the drop of a hat? If your character's identity was strongly linked to what it is they have lost, the impact can be more significant.

You can also reflect on how essential the pre-loss activity or role was to the character feeling 'good enough' as a person. Let's take the example of someone diagnosed with a significant illness whose mobility and energy will be permanently affected. For those with a fairly positive, secure self-view such as 'I'm good enough' and 'I'm loveable' these beliefs may remain relatively stable despite their painful loss. However, for another character who believes 'I'm not good enough or loveable unless I help others / earn money / prove myself all the time' their world may seem to crash down harder as they can't rely on their old ways of feeling sufficient anymore.

Task 8

*What does the loss represent to your character?

*Does it fundamentally change their view of themselves or the future somehow?

*Did your character's self-esteem depend on a role or activity they no longer have?

If so, how can you summarise that using the format 'I'm no longer good enough now that I'm not... or I can't... or I don't have...'

Grief and managing or experiencing losses can change with time. Your character may move between different presentations of grief. These don't happen in a set order from start to end but flow between states. The way your character feels about themselves and their future may also change across the course of your story. An initial period of shock may move to a position where they carve out a new future or version of themselves.

Sometimes a character may have lost someone to death or withdrawal who was abusive or rejecting of them, for example a parent. The grief experience here may be more about acknowledging the loss of what they never had (such as a loving parent or intact family), rather than the loss of the actual person.

Guilt and Shame

We have everyday uses of words which are fine for informal settings but may not have the best specificity when you want to think clearly about your characters. Guilt and shame do have a lot in common and can co-exist. However, you may find it helpful to distinguish between whether your character is feeling shame or guilt, and if it is guilt, whether it's healthy guilt or not.

Shame is focused on perceived differences between the actual self and the ideal self. The character experiencing shame is likely to either withdraw or work towards becoming like the ideal self.

Shame often has historical roots that cause a person to have painful thoughts about being flawed, undeserving or unworthy. The character will focus on who they think they are compared to who they 'should' be.

'I feel shame at the way I can't spell and get my letters muddled, I'm not the way I should be at my age.'

Guilt is an unpleasant feeling about having done something wrong. The character will focus on what they have done or failed to do, and how this wasn't in line with their values or standards.

Guilt is related to behaviour, goals, thoughts or traits that a person believes they are responsible for. It involves a moral self-evaluation. The character experiencing guilt is likely to either try to make things better or to self-punish in some way.

'I feel guilty about how selfish I was in my teens and didn't appreciate how hard my mum worked as a single parent. I like to make a big deal of Mother's day now.'

Task 9

*Does your character feel shame or guilt, or both?

*How does it show itself in thoughts and behaviour?

Guilt can be healthy or not. It's an important development in childhood to help us know when we have done something wrong and to increase the chances of that getting repaired in our social relationships. There could be good reason why your character feels guilty, for example if they harmed someone on purpose. The discomfort of guilt can lead a character to take responsibility for the harm and do something to try to make amends. Or your character may avoid that discomfort and use a defence mechanism such as blaming someone else which we will look at later.

Unhealthy guilt is when a person hasn't done anything wrong but blames themselves anyway or the guilt is far exaggerated compared to a minor harm done.

Task 10

*If your character feels shame about an aspect of themselves, where does this come from?

If you're not sure, can you add something into their past experiences to make sense of it?

*If your character has something to feel guilty about, do they acknowledge that and move to act or use some method to get rid of the feeling?

Is there change across time in them taking action to repair or are they somehow stuck in it?

*Does your character experience unhealthy guilt that is unfair to themselves?

If so, what has led to that pattern?

Jealousy and Envy

Two more concepts that get used interchangeably in everyday language but are in fact different are jealousy and envy. In basic terms, jealousy is 'I want to have that *person* instead of you' and envy is 'I want to have that *thing* instead of you'.

Envy often involves two people where one person lacks something that the other has. It is not inevitable in a situation where someone else has something valued (this could result in pleasure on their behalf, for example). However, for someone experiencing envy, it is linked to feelings of hostility toward the other person. Envy is often not socially acceptable so may be deliberately hidden or unconsciously changed into something else.

Jealousy usually involves three people, where one is concerned that they will lose out to a rival. Babies as young as five months old can display jealousy. Fear of abandonment is a key driver. Being prone to jealousy may link to early experiences such as sibling rivalry for parental attention. The more extreme end of jealousy will be seen more often in characters who have high anxiety around relationships and abandonment as we will discuss in the section on attachment.

Task 11

*If your character experiences envy, have you worked out why it is that particular thing they are envious about with that particular person?

How aware are they of their envious feelings?

*If your character experiences jealousy, do you have a reasonable account of why they would be prone to it? If not, could you add that to help your understanding of their development?

*Consider how you want your audience to feel towards your character.

Are scenes relating to envy or jealousy written in a way that will seem recognisable and understandable?

Do you want the reader to feel empathy or negative judgement towards this character? Does this match the way you have written about envy / jealousy?

Angels and Devils

Imagine a cartoon character with a devil on one shoulder telling him to steal what he wants and an angel on the other trying to rein him in. The poor character in the middle is pulled one way and another. You may have heard of the Id as the part of the self that is pleasure-seeking and impulsive in responding to desires. On the other side is the Super-ego which has rules based on early parenting and society. It warns the character to behave as society dictates and can cause feelings of unease or distress when less than perfect is achieved. Your character's Ego is the realistic part of the mind that tries to mediate between the two.

If your character had a background of punitive parenting and strong moral guidance in society about what is acceptable for them, the Super-ego / Angel aspect of the mind may be dominant. This character would feel guilt and shame, have high moral standards for self and others, and not accept normal, healthy feelings and longings.

If your character wasn't helped in their early years to wait for things, was spoiled or powerful in their relationships with instant gratification, they would develop an overly dominant Id / Devil. This can cause severe problems with relationships, antisocial or criminal behaviour and anger outbursts at anything and anyone that thwarts them.

You may find it helpful to consider the balance in your character and how successful they are at finding workable solutions to the pull between immediate gratification and strict disallowing.

Task 12

*Draw your character with their Super-ego/ Angel and Id /Devil in proportion to how influential each is.

*Label the types of drives and desires attached to the Id / Devil and what rules and restrictions come from the Superego / Angel.

*Does your character's parenting history and experience in society match the pattern you have drawn out?

Attachment Relationships

One of the main ways we learn what to think about ourselves is through the mirror of other people's reactions to us.

The first three years of your character's life will be highly influential in how they see themselves and what they expect from other people. Although not set in stone, the attachment patterns that develop during this period often show themselves across a person's life. They become more pronounced at times of stress such as an inciting incident for your character. Although you may never refer to those early years in your story, if you have figured it out for your character then you can check for consistency across time. If you need your character to change how they manage being in relationships, it should help you avoid moving too quickly or unrealistically across the story.

Patterns of relating to close others can be identified by looking at how young children are treated in childhood and the long-lasting implications of this. Let's consider possible experiences and their impact, taking care to remember these are normal variations not attachment 'disorders'. Don't worry if you recognise yourself in the insecure patterns – welcome to the club of around 40% of us.

In a secure attachment pattern, the parent met the child's needs in a sensitive and appropriate way most of the time. The infant experienced reliability and good care. Babies who are picked up and soothed when they cry actually show LESS crying a few months later than those who aren't. This is because the parent soothing them helps them to develop their own self-soothing. These securely attached toddlers are happy to explore what's around them as long as a parent is in sight. They feel safe and capable, trusting a caregiver to step up if needed. As adults, they have learnt to feel positive about other people and themselves in friendships and romantic relationships.

Let's look at the insecure attachment patterns and how they develop. This is just a framework – real life is far less clear-cut than the boxes suggest but it can be useful as an overall model.

Task 13

*The table below is designed to be read from left to right, across both pages. Which of these insecure attachment patterns seems the closest fit for your character?

Attachment Pattern	Child
Preoccupied Pattern Parent meets child's needs inconsistently e.g. parent uses substances or is sometimes very ill.	Learns to turn the dial up on behaviours such as clinging, neediness or tantrums to get or keep parental attention.
Dismissive Pattern Parent is absent, promotes self-reliance, withdraws if child shows high emotion or need.	Learns to look after themselves, not to rely on others, not to make a fuss.
Fearful Pattern Parent is frightening or frightened.	No set pattern of behaviour helps to protect the child or makes them feel safe.

ADULT	SELF / OTHER BELIEFS
Main focus is on other people. Main fear is abandonment. May be clingy, jealous, pleasing, does what it takes to keep a relationship.	Others are better than me. I need them.
Main focus is on independence and self. Main fear is being smothered by others. May keep people at arm's length, prefers to feel in control. Doesn't tend to show high emotions.	I'm better than others. I don't need them.
Combination of wanting intimacy but being too fearful of it. Pull / push in relationships. Poor self control and emotional regulation.	I'm no good, others are no good. I need them but can't trust them.

From looking at the chart and reflecting on your character, you may realise some elements of your story don't add up. We will discuss change in attachment patterns later.

Task 14

*If there are some inconsistencies or gaps in your character's adult presentation or child experiences, what do you need to rework?

Rules

An interesting technique to look at your character's internal world is to figure out how they think they should behave via rules. These internal rules are elicited by certain triggers that tell the character what they should do. Maybe you would expect a character to have insight into the rules and expectations they put onto themselves and others? Well, think again. Your character may never stop to think about WHY it's important to 'look after number one' or 'put others first' or 'keep going until your drop'. They may not even know that they have that rule because it will just seem like a self-evident fact that everyone should live by.

Consider the difference then in emotions and behaviour of two characters when there's a trigger of a shortage of toilet rolls announced on the local radio.

Character D's rule of 'look after number one' has him speeding down to the local shop to bulk buy for himself as that's an essential and totally acceptable part of survival to him.

Character E has the rule 'put others first' elicited, so starts to be careful with his toilet paper consumption and texts his family to warn them.

Two different rules lead to two different behaviours, that's understandable.

But hang on, what if Character E gets a huge jolt of anxiety at imagining his poor family suffering with no toilet paper? He too speeds down to the shop to stock up so that his elderly parents don't suffer, even though that puts him in the uncomfortable position of jostling for the last mega-pack with Character D.

Here we have the SAME behaviour but from following DIFFERENT rules, and possibly with different emotional states. Character D is angry at everyone in his way and Character E is anxious about letting his loved ones down.

The example shows you that a character's behaviour isn't enough in itself to give true insight. You need to consider and show their internal world of rules, beliefs, emotions, intentions and so on. That's what will differentiate clearly between your characters.

Here's a way to think about these 'rules'

I should… otherwise…

I shouldn't… otherwise…

So our two very different characters' rules could be written as:

D - I should look after number one, otherwise I'll suffer.

E - I shouldn't put myself first, otherwise I'm a bad person

Task 15

*Take one or two scenes from your story where something significant happens.

What internal rules get triggered (in the format I should / shouldn't, otherwise…)?

How does that impact on your character's behaviour?

Does this rule occur more than once across the story to help build up a sense of character for the reader?

Are there hints to the reader about the character's point of view or rules, even if the character themselves is not aware?

*And if you want to dig deeper:

WHY does your character have this set of rules in particular? Where do they come from e.g. parents, school, media, religion, etc.

Thinking Habits

Our brains have evolved shortcuts in thinking which can be effective time and energy savers. However, they also put us at risk of making assumptions that don't match reality. Here are some examples that may be relevant to explain why your character thinks or acts the way they do.

Confirmation bias

Your character may search for, pay more attention to and better recall information that supports what they already believe. This may cause delay in your character noticing and processing any evidence that goes against their belief, such as figuring out their partner is the murderer.

Self-Serving Bias

Your character may put successes down to personal reasons but failures down to external reasons. This protective bias may prevent a character from taking responsibility when things have gone wrong as they don't look at their own role in the failure.

Optimism Bias

Your character may over-estimate the probability that good things will happen to them and underestimate how likely negative things are to happen to them. This may then influence their behaviour such as risk-taking.

Halo Effect

Your character may assume that because someone is good or strong in one area, they must be strong in other unrelated areas. Physical attractiveness in someone may lead to presumptions that the person is also good, kind, clever, wouldn't commit a crime, and so on.

Dunning-Kruger Effect

If your character is bad at something they may believe they are much more capable at it than they are. Their confidence in themselves is a poor measure of ability.

Task 16

*Are there thinking biases in your character that shape the way they make sense of the world and how they act?

(They may be on the list or not).

*If so, have you helped the reader to understand the difference between their thinking bias and reality in your story?

Next, we will look at negative thinking habits. Any character (or person, let's face it), can experience these at times. However, if your character has poor self-esteem, insecure attachment, low mood or anxiety, or a history of trauma, they may be more likely to show a number of them and more often. By being clear what thinking habits your character is prone to, you can take care to match this to their speech, skewed thinking and focus within the story.

Task 17

*Do any of these negative thinking habits fit for your character and how is that shown within your story?

Filtering
Your character focusses on the negative details and filters out the positive.

Jumping to Conclusions
Your character jumps to conclusions about what someone else is feeling or thinking about them without evidence.

Personalisation
Your character thinks that what other people do or say is a direct reaction to them, taking everything personally.

Fortune Telling
Your character believes they know what will happen in the future and it will be bad.

Negative Labels
Your character has a negative belief about themselves and applies it to everything e.g. I'm useless.

Compare and Despair
Your character sees only the positive in other people, comparing themselves negatively against them.

Emotional Reasoning
Your character believes if they feel something (such as jealousy that their partner is cheating) then it must be true.

Overgeneralisation
Your character takes one negative experience and expects that means it will continue to happen such as a fall-out with one friend meaning they can never have a lasting friendship.

You may start to see links between previous sections and these thinking patterns. Behaviours, mood and relationships may all be impacted by the types of thinking your character tends to fall into, and more so at times of threat or stress.

Task 18

*How might the thinking biases and / or negative thinking habits impact on your character's interactions with other characters?

Armour

There are likely to be drivers for your character's behaviour that come from self-protection EVEN IF those behaviours end up making life harder.

For example, a character may put up with awful behaviours from someone as a way to protect themselves from that person's rage or abandonment. Another character might be unkind and rejecting to someone they are in love with to protect themselves from the pain of it all going wrong.

For this topic of armour, I'm asking you to consider the things that your character does to protect themselves from perceived risk of harm. They may or may not be aware of why they do these things or the fact that they are on some level done for self-protection.

We will think more broadly about coping strategies and defence mechanisms later.

Task 19

*What armour does your character wear?

(e.g. a behaviour they do, how they react to others, what they avoid, common phrases they use to PROTECT themselves from perceived harm or distress)

*What do they do it to protect themselves from, even though they may not realise it?

(e.g. rejection, pain, loss, being disappointed)

Coping

Coping techniques can be thought of as the things our characters choose to do ON PURPOSE to help them manage something challenging. We will discuss later defence mechanisms which are unconscious (so not chosen or on purpose).

There's no clear divide between what is a 'good' or 'bad' coping technique. An action that is helpful at one point (I'll stop getting stressed about this and go for a walk instead) could be effective in one circumstance (revising for an exam) and unhelpful in another (taking the exam).

It can be interesting to look at the range of coping strategies your character uses when things get tricky. Some may have become habitual and preventative rather than waiting for things to go wrong.

Emotion-focused coping aims to reduce the negative emotional impact of stress.

Problem-focused coping aims to tackle the actual problem that caused stress.

Coping styles can be categorised into groups that a particular person may be more likely to use.

Task 20

*Tick off for your character their main ways of dealing with stress or challenges.

TYPE OF COPING	EXAMPLE
Wishful thinking	Hope a miracle will happen or the problem will go away somehow
Escape-avoidance	Sleep more than usual or eat and drink more to feel better
Social support	Talk to someone about it or seek professional help
Self-controlling	Try to keep feelings in
Aggressive	Fight for what they want or express anger to the person who caused it
Problem-solving	Come up with solutions or draw on past experiences
Accept responsibility	Do something to make amends or criticise self

Patterns of coping don't arise in a vacuum. There are influences including what people see their family and peers do, what is deemed 'appropriate' for them from a cultural perspective, what they have access to, and what the unspoken expectations were as they grew up. For example, in families where nobody 'makes a fuss' a character may be more likely to use practical or avoidant strategies whereas another character who grew up in a time and place where social support was the norm would be more likely to reach out to others.

Task 21

*Can you account for WHY your character uses the coping strategies that they do?

If not, can you work backwards and create some reasons that fit?

You could try asking questions such as:

Where did the character learn to do this?

What are the maintenance factors that keep them doing this type of coping again and again?

What are the barriers to your character switching to a different way of coping?

* Does anything not fit across the story in terms of how your character copes with stress or challenge?

If they suddenly use very different types of coping, is there reason for that change?

Perception

Do I see what you see? No. We construct and make sense of what we see based on filters that lead us to notice, interpret, recall and experience the same situation differently. You can consider this as the 'glasses' your character wears, from the rosiest pink to the darkest sunglasses.

Let's say your character is sitting at a bar when the bartender says that their drink has been paid for by someone else. How would your character react?

That depends on many factors such as presumptions about what it means, how safe they feel, what they have learnt about whether to trust others, and so on. It may also depend on something that happened that day – did the local newspaper report about drinks being spiked or twenty percent of new relationships starting through an act of kindness?

What you may notice is there are some general features about your character that will influence how they act (e.g. what they have learnt about trusting other people).

But there will also be situational factors that are relevant such as what has happened that day, what mood they are in, whether the setting triggers a memory, what they overheard recently, and so on.

It can therefore be useful to have an overall idea of the 'glasses' your character views the world through, but also to consider carefully in a scene what particular aspects may be triggered which might impact their responses.

Task 22

*Think about the 'glasses' your character tends to perceive the world through

(e.g. Rosy – thinks the best of other people and themselves or Grey – checks for danger, aims to protect themselves as a priority).

*Now take a key scene in your story where something significant happens. What 'filters' is your character seeing things through? Try to focus on specifics as below:

Beliefs about themselves and other people
Role they have taken on in the scene
Emotions during this scene
Rules that have been triggered
Any memories that the event has triggered
Any sense of threat that has been triggered
Any hidden longing that has been triggered

*In what way have any of those filters influenced how your character has experienced the situation or how they responded?

Values

Knowing what your character's values are can help you retain a realistic focus for them and differentiate them from other characters.

Your character's values are not the same as their goals. Goals are specific and have an end-point once the goal is reached. Values are more like a path than a destination – they provide purpose and meaning to the character (when they are acknowledged and used to guide them).

Task 23

*Consider the following areas of values and work out how highly your character would rate each in terms of how important it is to them with 0 being not at all to 10 being very important.

Relationships (Family, partners, friendships)
Parenting
Community / helping others
Work, training or education
World / environment

Hobbies / Interests / Enjoyment
Religion / spirituality
Leaving a legacy behind
Physical Health
Mental wellbeing / personal growth

Not living according to values can cause dissatisfaction and a lack of a sense of purpose. Living closely aligned to values can be protective at times of stress or change as they can provide a 'compass' for your character of how to act (e.g. according to values to be loving or creative) even if goals get trampled (e.g. relationship ends or fatigue prevents completing a project).

Task 24

*Are there areas that your character scored highly on as strongly valued but they are not living by at the start of the story?

*What gets in the way of them living by their values or using them as a compass to guide what they do?

We will consider any change in how much your character lives by their values in a later section.

Longings

You'll need your shovel for this section.

The driver of a story is often the longings of the main character. You may have a character who longs to make it as a 1930s Hollywood starlet, or to prove to their boss they can solve the crime better than their sleazy colleague, or to save everyone on the Mars explorer pod before they run out of oxygen. Or gentler longings like to find themselves by escaping to village life.

These can hold true while still inviting the possibility to also dig underneath and search for the meaning of that longing in your character. This additional depth can produce a satisfactory and emotionally engaging experience for the reader.

Typical healthy longings include the longing to connect, to give and receive love, to be heard and understood, for intimacy and sexual relationships, for play and joy.

A method that can help you to get to the meaning of the longing for your character is to probe and ask clarifying questions about longings.

Let's try with one of the examples above.

What does the character long for?
    She wants to make it as a Hollywood star.

What would it mean to her if she did make it?
    That she would be known, famous and admired.

Why is it so important for her to be known and admired?
    It would make her feel good and successful.

If she felt successful, what would that mean to her?
    That she was accepted, had proved herself.

Why do you think it's important to this character to feel accepted or to prove herself?
    I suppose she always wanted to feel accepted but never did.

Are there reasons in this character's past that explain why acceptance is important to her?
    Yes, she was ignored by her parents and told she'd never amount to anything. She never fitted in.

So, it sounds like her longing to be a star links to a deeper yearning to be noticed and accepted in a way she missed out on when she was younger?

In this example, you could also explore why the fantasy is about being a Hollywood star in particular, rather than another route to becoming accepted and loved by many.

If you were to speak to this character, would she recognise the deeper longing for attention and love? Or would she dismiss it, saying that she simply wants to use her acting skills?

Your character may be aware of the deeper longings or they could be outside of awareness – too painful or unacceptable to acknowledge.

Task 25

*What does your character long for in the story (in the most obvious or practical way)?

*If you're not already aware of why the longing is meaningful to your character, where it came from, and why it takes the form it does, try investigating the matter with probing questions as above.

There may be some instances where the apparent longing and hidden longing are in fact very different. For example, a character who appears to long for an admirer to leave them alone when actually under the surface they have longings to connect, be loved and settle down. Look at chapters on self-sabotage, anxiety, rules and attachment for some ideas about why this might be the case.

It's worth considering whether your character's journey involves them becoming aware of the hidden aspect or not. However, you do want the reader to follow clues even if the character remains in the dark, so they can understand and build empathy. We will look at the trajectory of both character and reader gaining awareness in Part 3.

Task 26

*Is there an aspect of healthy longing that your character is unaware of?

*Why have they learnt to hide it?

*What do they do or experience instead of noticing or acting on this longing?

Defence Mechanisms

Imagine I've borrowed the Truth Mirror from the Evil Queen. It told her Snow White was the fairest in the land – a truth she knew unconsciously but didn't want to accept. That answer triggered a painful realisation in the Queen. It hurt. She automatically pushed it down. So she acted out by poisoning Snow White with an apple to help regain her sense of being special.

Defence mechanisms can be thought about as the thing your character does when a glance into the Truth Mirror of their real feelings and longings threatens to overwhelm them. It's a way their minds automatically put something into place that distracts from, skews or diverts away from a painful reality when it comes into conscious awareness.

If your character is relatively robust (with a decent view of themselves and others, an ability to self-soothe, skills to cope with the world's challenges and so on), then they may use a defence mechanism that's relatively healthy and doesn't significantly skew reality.

Let's say Snow White hears that the Evil Queen is kicking off about her again. She gets a flash of healthy anger about it but that doesn't sit comfortably with her belief that she shouldn't waste her time on negative people and her desire to focus on her community. So, at the allotment with her animal friends she yanks out weeds and stomps on them, redirecting her anger into a pro-social task. This is a defence mechanism rather than a coping strategy because Snow White is unaware of the link between her triggered anger at the Queen and her enthusiastic weed-stomping.

Here are some examples of defence mechanisms at the end of a spectrum that is relatively healthy and doesn't warp reality too much. These focus more on redirection and distraction:

- Being assertive
- Focusing on a strength
- Making a joke out of it
- Imagining things turning out well in the future

Then there are defence mechanisms which move a bit further from reality in order to block the rising feeling, for example:

- Trying to 'undo' a hurt or bad feeling towards someone by being extra nice to them afterwards
- Saying that a failure or hurt was for the best
- Intellectualising about something awful that has happened
- Turning the feeling onto someone else who didn't trigger it where it's safer (such as arguing with a spouse rather than the manager)

Finally, there are defence mechanisms that turn the Truth Mirror into a Hall of Mirrors instead, bending reality without realising it. Characters who use these defences are more likely to have major struggles in managing their own emotions, with more significant problems with how they feel about themselves and others, and who often feel under threat.

- Projecting their own undesirable thoughts and feelings onto someone else
- Dissociation in which they don't feel real, lose chunks of time or feels disconnected
- Acting out in an extreme way such as hurting others or themselves
- Denying to themselves what is evidently true

Remember your character uses a defence mechanism immediately following a disallowed feeling, thought or longing being triggered. In your scene, make sure that this is clear to show the reader what the painful aspect is. Your character will not know why they are acting that way, it is automatic and unconscious.

Task 27

*Look back at your list of hidden feelings and longings for your character.

Find or create a scene in which one gets triggered and see what level of defence mechanism fits for your character here.

*How much does your character tend to warp reality when hidden feelings are triggered?

*Check that you are satisfied that any defence mechanisms that occur have a clear trigger.

There may be some scenes where a defence mechanism fails to work and your character is faced with the truth of their feeling or longing instead. This can be the first step to insight and change as we will discuss later.

Part 2: The Specifics

Teenagers

The teenage brain is not yet fully developed. Changes take place during adolescence and beyond that may be useful to be aware of for a younger character's behaviour.

One of the last areas to develop at the front of the brain relates to planning, prioritising and controlling impulses. The judgment area of the brain develops into the early twenties, making it more of a challenge for teenagers than adults to properly risk-assess their behaviour. They have poorer 'brakes' to stop themselves acting on what they want. This is particularly hard during stressful times.

Teenage brains need more 'rewards' than adults to feel excitement so they may go for more thrill-seeking activities to get a kick. They are less able than adults to think through possible consequences of their behaviour.

The hormone surges in puberty can have a significant impact on the emotional centre of the brain. This can be one factor in mood swings. Teens may feel overwhelmed by situations such as a fallout with friends or a partner with less ability to think things through clearly. They are also poorer than adults at reading facial expressions accurately, meaning they may misinterpret someone else's feelings.

The sleep pattern of teenagers shifts so that their sleep hormone increases later at night and drops later in the morning than when they were younger. Most teens don't get the level of sleep they need (9- 10 hours) which can further impact their mood and behaviour.

Task 28

*Are any of these facts about the teenage brain relevant to your character and if so, how?

*What are other influences specific to the teenage period for your character (either now if they are a young person or looking back to when they were a teenager), building on what we learned earlier in this book

(e.g. learnt behaviour, disallowed feelings for that age, shame, etc)

Family Roles

What roles does your character get pulled into on a one-to-one basis? They may behave like a mature, wise adult until they visit their grandmother or ex-partner or boss, at which point they could switch into a more child-like role. Or they meet one particular friend in a scene and become more like a parent to them.

Think about how your character relates to key other people. What role do they take with that particular person?

Parent-like

Adult-like

Child-like

These states happen with a particular person to create a pattern between the two of them.

For example

Adult – Adult (mature, equal relationship)

Parent – Child (one being critical of or nurturing towards one who is acting young)

Your character may be adult-like most of the time until they visit their brother who plays out a Child role. This pulls your character into Critical Parent role (just like they experienced when they were young).

This idea may help you figure out why or how your character is sometimes different with certain people. They may get pulled into old patterns of what they experienced in the past, particularly if the other person falls into a role that pulls them there.

Task 29

*Is there a key relationship where your character shifts in their role when they are with that person?

*What role does your character take and what is the other person's role using the parent / adult / child model?

*What impact or difference does it make when your character switches into this role?

Social Roles

We have already discussed your character's roles in a one-to-one context. Next, we can broaden out to consider the role they tend to take within a group of people.

For this task, I'm going to ask you to forget about your story. Peel your character off the page and place them into a totally new scenario. The aim of this is to reduce the possible limitations that come from being so clear about the needs of the story that you may not be paying attention to some aspects of character.

We are going to focus on how your character responds in the context of several other people being there when a group task is necessary. This will make you consider them in a wider social context.

Characters may have patterns of thinking and behaving when they are focused on their own business. But what happens when they have to interact with multiple others or when there are demands a single person can't sort out by themselves?

Let's take your character on a trip to an island. A group of twelve travellers has been marooned on the island and there will be no rescue boat for some time.

Task 30

*How does your character respond to this initially?

(e.g. is it a chance for escape, does it feel worrying, a waste of time, a puzzle to be solved, a competition to win?)

*What would your character prioritise in the first few days?

(e.g. comfort, friendship, dominance, reflecting on how they got here, preparing for the next day, trying to get home despite being told there's no boat?)

What does that say about them?

REFLECTION: Do any of the above answers surprise you or is this just how they act in their own world?

If you're not sure of any answers it might flag up an area to spend a little time on.

On this island there's a sandy beach where the travellers can hang out, some trees for shade, and a mountain to climb. Food has to be caught from the sea or picked from the trees. Here are some examples of the types of roles your character may take as the group members have to work out how to feed and shelter themselves.

Task-focused roles e.g. coming up with ideas, seeking information or others' opinions, evaluating if the ideas are workable.

Social roles e.g. encouraging others, making sure everyone has a voice, agreeing, or harmonising tensions between group members.

Dysfunctional roles e.g. making personal attacks, blocking or discrediting everyone's ideas, making it about themselves, dominating or acting helpless to gain sympathy.

Task 31

*Where would your character want to spend time while stuck on the island?

Does this differ from what they'd actually do because of there being other people present?

*What would others expect from your character if they made snap judgements based on the way your character looks and acts?

*From the list of group roles, what fits best with what you would expect your character to do when the group has to decide on how to get food and stay safe?

Your character exists in a certain context for your story, but it can be helpful to think about how they tend to act and what role they take around other people. You may like to think about your own story and how some of these group roles already show up or where it might be useful to include them if relevant to your story.

Trauma

Trauma is an emotional response to a distressing experience. This might be a one-off incident like being in a car accident or ongoing harm such as years of bullying. Although some people reach the level of a post-traumatic stress disorder (PTSD) diagnosis, many people will show some symptoms of trauma in the short-term after a frightening experience which resolve.

Responses to trauma vary from one person to another. Here are some possible reactions following a traumatic experience:

- A character's beliefs about themselves and the world may change, for example a shift from feeling competent in a safe world to feeling vulnerable in a dangerous world.
- Emotional reactions may include increased anxiety, anger, confusion or a sense of numbness.
- The character may experience nightmares, invasive thoughts about what happened or flashbacks which feel like going back in time and reliving the event.
- Bodily changes may include feeling on edge, fatigue and heightened jumpiness or agitation.
- Behaviours may change to becoming avoidant of any possible reminders of what happened.
- Self-blame or shame may be triggered.

Task 32

*What has been the impact of trauma on your character in the following areas:

- What they think about themselves, others or the world
- Feeling overwhelmed with emotions or numbness
- Experiencing reliving such as flashbacks or nightmares
- Avoiding triggers
- Bodily changes such as the overarousal symptoms described in the anxiety chapter

*Are there factors which help your character's symptoms of trauma to reduce over time?

(e.g. support network, self care, self-regulation, realising they were not to blame)

Narcissism

If you have a narcissistic character in your story you may find it useful to consider what lies beneath the apparent self-belief.

A narcissistic character will act as if they are superior to everyone else. They believe they should be revered and get what they want without any effort as they are special. They have superficial relationships that exist only to gain admiration.

However, this can be viewed as a 'mask' that the character wears to protect themselves. Underneath, they are fragile with an intense focus on how others view them. They can't tolerate being a 'normal' person who may make mistakes, not be highly regarded by everyone or show any needs. They constantly belittle others and seek praise in order to avoid any painful truths getting through about their lack of 'special' status.

If this sounds like your character, then they may have ended up that way through two different paths. One is a spoilt child who was given everything, not taught limits or to follow rules, and lavishly praised by parents despite making no effort. They learnt to expect to be treated as 'special' which is not how the real world operates. The other path is those who couldn't meet the high expectations of their parents and learnt to cover their shame at feeling not good enough by lying, boasting and inventing the mask of being 'special'.

Task 33

*If you have a character with narcissistic qualities, does your story show their intense focus on others' view of them?

*Do you have or could you add key scenes that show a time when the reality of them not being 'special' threatens to rise to awareness, so they step up their narcissistic behaviours or use another defence mechanism to avoid this?

*Considering the two pathways to narcissim that were described, what was the route to your character developing these traits?

Perfectionism

Perfectionism involves a striving towards flawlessness. Your character may show varying degrees. At the mild end of striving to do well this may help to motivate them. At the more severe end they could become significantly distressed and their life severely impacted.

It is impossible for anyone to be 'perfect' so this trait inevitably sets people up to be unable to meet their own harsh standards. This perceived failure can then lead to further striving so that the character gets caught in a loop of hard work and disappointment. For some characters, they may end up using other self-sabotaging behaviours such as procrastination or avoidance. Without necessarily being aware of it, there could be an underlying belief such as 'if I never finish this project, it won't be judged as failing.'

Your character's perfectionist tendencies may link back to experiences of harsh judgement, conditional love, or high focus on achievement in the family, education and social context. The character may struggle to notice or accept compliments as their perceived standards have not been met. Successes could be put down to luck, poor judgement or somebody being kind.

It may be hard for your character to keep hold of any sense of satisfaction in what they have achieved before their attention turns to the next day, task or person to please.

Task 34

*If your character has perfectionist traits, how do those show up in the story?

Does it link to other thoughts, behaviour patterns or self-sabotage as discussed in other chapters?

*In what ways has perfectionism motivated your character and how has it been unhelpful?

*Where does the unrealistic drive for perfection come from for your character?

*Have you shown how they react to success, compliments or positivity from others?

Work and Leisure

What your character chooses to do for work or leisure can give clues about them as a person. However, remember the warning about the 'dream dictionary'? Rather than deciding what a certain type of character is likely to do, it can be helpful to dig in a little more to consider the FUNCTION of that work or hobby for them.

Let's take the example of a job as a nurse.

Character F has a secure attachment style, thinks positively about herself, values helping others and enjoys being part of a wider team sharing the purpose of best care for patients. That fits with nursing, right?

Now consider Character G. He has a preoccupied attachment style so prefers to feel needed at work with lots of close contact with people. Other people knowing he is a nurse helps him to feel better about himself as it's a role that is valued in his community. He finds it hard to turn down extra shifts in case that means letting people down. He's known as a great team player and often brings food in for his colleagues to keep them liking him and spends extra time with patients after his shift has ended. Still fits with nursing then?

And finally, Character H. She has an avoidant attachment style. She likes there to be clear rules and processes that should be followed where everyone knows their place in a hierarchy. She is confident in her ability to get her job done correctly and double checks everyone else's work. With perfectionist traits, she leads on infection control initiatives so is seen by the team as an expert. Long hours mean she avoids social demands with the valid excuse of working. A different kind of feel to it than the others but still a possible good fit for nursing?

Of course, characters don't always get the choice to have the job or career they want. However, you can still consider what your character gets from their work and why they do their job in a certain way.

You can repeat the process when thinking about hobbies. Yes, there may be certain leisure activities more likely for one character than another, but it is still helpful to consider the WHY or FUNCTIONS of that behaviour.

Task 35

*In what ways does the specific work or leisure activity of your character fit with what you know about them?

*What does their work / leisure mean to them?

*How might other characters or the reader get to understand them through the way that they approach their work or leisure?

Meaning

Humans are made to find meaning. We are built in a way that triggers us to create connections between things. If you're willing to play, read on.

Task 36

*Think of a random object.

I want you to think of one way in which your object is similar to a dolphin. It doesn't matter how you link them but you MUST think of a way.

Can you think of why I may have chosen a dolphin specifically for YOU? What was the meaning of that? In what way was I communicating to you by choosing a dolphin...?

It doesn't matter what object you thought of, your mind can probably come up with ways to link our words even if that has to be quite bizarre. And you may have found a personal link to the word dolphin, too.

When you think about it, it's no surprise that minds may link an object, place, sound, series of events, a tingling sensation at the back of the neck, frolics of a certain number of black and white birds in the garden, and so on, to the one constant – the self.

Your character may look for meaning without realising it, just as a child can see familiar shapes in the clouds. They have a brain that is wired to make connections and see patterns of similarity and meaning.

To your main character, the story really is all about them. They can't help it. It's how we are made. This allows you to display some of your character's internal world by what they see, notice, link to, guess at, misattribute or react to in the external world of the story.

What shape do you think a character is more likely to see in the clouds if they have been trying to start a family for three years? What would they notice in the street or the supermarket? What could they think it means if a flyer for an IVF clinic blows past at the bus stop? Sometimes stories are criticised for relying on unbelievable coincidence but that doesn't take account of the fact that this character didn't notice a flier for pizza delivery because that didn't link emotionally in the same way.

If you have a character who is jealous or struggling to decide what to do next, they may well look for the 'answers' that they already expect or want. Let the reader see the world through the eyes of the character. This can work particularly well if you are writing about the same events from multiple points of view or you have a passive character who wants to avoid taking responsibility for their choices and actions.

Task 37

*Are there ways in which your character searches for or finds answers outside of themselves?

(e.g. reading signs in the natural world, superstition, making links between unrelated things, feeling part of a predesigned plan)

*If so, what do they get out of doing this? Does it help or hold them back in any ways?

*How can the reader learn more about the character from the way in which they see signs or meaning around them?

Self-Sabotage

Our poor characters have to be thwarted in multiple ways in order to have an arc to a story. Sometimes the barriers will be external but in real life they are often internal.

If your character is one who self-sabotages, they may not realise it. Their choices and behaviours repeatedly get in the way of what they want or need. However, your character may have a completely different way of looking at things, as if there was no other choice or it was the 'right' thing to do.

Here are some examples:

Procrastination – they put off submitting their job application for so long that they lose out on the chance of a dream job (*cough, write your book, cough*)

Walking away – they end friendships or romantic relationships at the first sign of disagreement, telling themselves it will inevitably fail so it's better to get out early.

Avoidance – they don't do the things they love, stating they don't have the time.

These unhelpful patterns ultimately stop the character getting their own wishes. The outcome may well match a part of their mind that tells them they don't deserve or are not good enough for a career / relationship / joy and so on. Or it could be part of the armour – don't try and then you can't feel the pain of failing. There's likely to be a background of low self-esteem and self-punishing thoughts that came from early experiences of being treated as if they were not deserving or good enough.

Task 38

*Are you clear about whether the barriers your character faces in the story are external, internal or what combination of the two?

*If your character self-sabotages, how does this show itself?

*Can their self-sabotage be understood in line with their history or could you add more backstory in your plans to make sense of this behaviour?

Pleasers

Your character may be someone who is warm, helpful and always doing their best for others. That in itself is not a problem and may link to their values. However, for some characters the drive to prioritise others leads them to ignore or diminish their own needs. Rather than seeing others as equally important and deserving as themselves, they may see everyone else's needs as valuable and their own as disallowed.

Pleasers may be aware of a rule they have that they must keep others happy. For example, they may fear repercussions such as violence or abandonment if they don't focus on what others need.

For other pleasers, they have spent so long putting everyone else's needs above their own, they no longer have a sense of what they want, or maybe even who they are.

If your character is at this more extreme end of being a pleaser, they may be unaware of or push down their own emotional, social and perhaps even basic physical needs (such as for having enough to drink, eat and rest).

You may see links between this kind of pleasing pattern and the preoccupied attachment pattern, a 'rule' that 'I should focus on others, otherwise…', and a tendency to disallow healthy anger that prevents them putting in healthy boundaries.

In terms of wearing 'armour', for some characters it is almost as if the protective armour is so tight that it prevents signals from the body travelling up to awareness in the mind that the character has their own needs.

For some pleasers, they may become very resentful about others not realising how hard they work, what their needs are, not asking them if they are okay, not noticing their distress or pain. They may not realise that by always acting 'okay' and running around after everyone else, they are sabotaging their chances of being cared for and understood.

Task 39

*If your character is a pleaser, where have you shown this in the story so it's clear (i.e. that it is imbalanced with how they treat themselves rather than just being kind)?

*How aware are they of this pattern?

*What does this pleasing pattern link to in their rules, attachment history or emotional world?

*Are you clear how this pattern has developed and what keeps it going for this character?

Part 3: Putting it All Together

Digging into Character

Here's an example of what it might look like if I question someone about a character in a way to help them get below the surface. (There are some similarities to questions that may be asked in therapy to help someone discover more about themselves). You can use this as a framework to think about any aspect of your character's behaviour or thinking.

How does your character view himself?
He thinks he's invincible, better than everyone else.

Let's think about what lies underneath that. What does it achieve for him to think that way?
I think it helps him feel strong and good about himself, and it pushes him to succeed.

It sounds like he works hard to ensure he feels better than others. What would happen if he stopped telling himself and others that he's better?
Oh. I don't know. He'd feel bad?

Why would he feel bad if he couldn't prove he was better than others?
Well then maybe they'd see he isn't better, he's no different to them.

And why would that be so bad for him – for people to see him as the same as them?

Maybe he'd worry he wouldn't be strong and in charge anymore.

What would he fear could happen if he wasn't strong or in charge?

I wonder if he'd worry that if he's not seen as in charge, people might walk over him or ignore him.

Why do you think this character in particular has a fear that he might be ignored or mistreated if he isn't in control?

Well… I guess that's how his dad was with him, a bully who never really gave him time or positive attention. He must have hated being ignored by his dad, but also fearful he would set off dad's anger.

So on the surface your character tells himself he's better than everyone but it seems like underneath the surface he has a hidden fear that he's not special and will get ignored or even harmed if he doesn't behave this way, that it could make him vulnerable?

Hmm. Maybe.

What difference would it make to your reader if they got to see that side?

I'll go and think about it…

So here are a few questions you could ask yourself about why your character behaves in the way they do:

Have they learnt that directly or indirectly from others?

Was that behaviour effective or protective somehow in the past?

What do they think would happen if they stopped that behaviour?

Why would that be so bad?

Why would this particular thing (e.g. loneliness, being noticed, getting something wrong, falling in love, getting angry, etc) be what is anxiety-provoking for your character, rather than something else?

If anything doesn't add up or isn't accounted for then you can adapt or invent to make it fit.

These questions are also really helpful when you are writing a character who does awful things. To reduce the risk of them being a one-dimensional bad guy, dig down to the drivers of their behaviour which may well show some hidden fears and longings.

Task 40

*You could use the list of questions as a paper exercise or pair up with another writer and interview each other about your characters.

If you get stuck, ask the other writer(s) to brainstorm some possibilities – sometimes this helps to shake you out of the shackles of your own experiences.

Perspective

Earlier we looked at different perceptions by considering what 'glasses' your character wears to interpret events. This can be particularly interesting if you have different characters relaying the same incidents. It doesn't mean one is lying, it means you've shown their experiences through their personal filters.

Writing in first person allows you to show the internal workings of your character to the reader. Let them see the inconsistencies, the self-deceit, show defence mechanisms in action and how real and true the rules seem for how to behave.

If you are writing in close third person, you can still give the reader a sense of being inside a character's mind. No description is neutral. If you are describing a room, you're making decisions about what to include or exclude. Put your character's 'glasses' on before you write – it will make a difference.

Let's imagine a scene at a beach. It's a warm day with a light breeze. There's a character lying on the sand, propped up on her elbows to face the sea as the water laps at her feet. How would this be described in third person? Your focus in description and the language you choose can help give insights into the character's internal world.

I'll describe the same waves differently for each of the three characters without needing to use first person. The short version is more subtle. If you add the section in brackets it's less subtle with more guidance for the reader, depending on what you need in a particular scene.

Character I
The gentle waves lapped at Ella's feet (in rhythm with her breath).

Character J
There was an urgency to the waves' pull (beckoning Ella towards the depths).

Character K
The shush of the waves was relentless (warning Ella to keep her secret).

Task 41

*What would be your guess about the internal world of each of these three characters?

Pay attention to what aspects of the sentence led to your conclusions.

If you took each of these characters in turn, you could make guesses from just one sentence about their state of mind, mood, beliefs about themselves, rules, level of threat perceived, and so on. As you build your story through the lens of your character, the reader will get to understand their world without you having to use excerpts from their diary or unrealistic conversation spilling all their history and concerns. You may find it interesting to see that not only what but HOW you have written gives clues to the reader about different topics we have covered in this book.

Task 42

Either:

*Take your character out of the story and place them on this beach. Write a paragraph that only describes the beach but would relay some of the core elements of your character's internal world.

(You don't need to say 'she notices...' just make the choice to describe the sand as invading her shoes or the layers of rock showing up in the cliffs.)

Or:

*Pick or develop a key scene in your story and check if the lens through which you are writing has given your reader any insight into the character without spoon-feeding them.

Change

This is the longest chapter in the book. Give yourself time to read through and see which element of change feels most relevant to your character.

We like our characters to change in some way over the course of a story. Sometimes in small ways, sometimes life-changing. We have discussed topics that may be useful to revisit in the context of what could change in your character over the course of your story.

Humans rarely change easily. However challenging things get, your character may find comfort in the familiar. You need to have steps leading to your character's change. The number and pacing of these will differ depending on the length of your writing.

Once you have identified one or two key areas of change or growth in your character, you can use the arc of your story to map out how the specific changes occur over time using trigger points in scenes. If you focus on a couple of main changes, it doesn't mean nothing else differs. What tends to happen is that one area of change – such as gaining trust in others – pulls along other changes as if they are tied on the same rope. So as the character gains trust, they also let their armour down, change their social role, act more in line with their values, and so on.

There are many suggestions below. You only need to focus on a couple that are most relevant to your character's change or growth over the story.

Attachment

Attachment patterns are formed in the first three years of life. They can be altered over time, for example through a nurturing adult romantic relationship. However, rather than thinking of characters switching to different styles it's more realistic to think about how they move within that style. So your character may start off as strongly dismissing, but be more on the mild side with secure elements by the end of the story. At times of high stress (such as an inciting incident), your character is likely to revert back to their old ways. They could be doing well in a stable friendship or relationship until threat rears up and they go back to old habits such as intense clinging, rejecting behaviour or lack of trust in everyone.

Task 43

*Across your story, does the character's attachment style change in how it presents at all?

*What were the key factors that allowed the change to happen? Have you shown or alluded to them over the arc of the story so the reader can see the pathway to change?

Rules

Rules don't tend to change overnight or disappear completely. However, they can be less frequently triggered or lose their power over time as new learning takes place.

Task 44

*Does your character loosen how tightly they grip onto some of their internal 'rules' or change them?

*Have you shown enough to account for this change? (e.g. how they tried out other ways of behaving or circumstances that pushed them to be more flexible)

Armour

Your character may change in the way they let down their guard a little, peel off an item of armour if you like. This doesn't tend to happen in real life by someone simply having a revelation of 'oh, I don't need to do that, I'll just stop'. You can consider ways in which they take one tiny bit of armour off at a time like a test.

A character who puts on 'armour' of being rejecting towards someone they are in love with may experiment on a small scale by acknowledging a thank you or sharing some food. This wouldn't happen out of the blue! Imagine a storyline of enemies to lovers where both parties have their armour on and don't acknowledge the attraction and longing. You may find them thrown into a situation where they must co-operate to survive a threat or solve a mystery. So slowly, slowly one little item of armour is relinquished –they share a drink or laugh at a joke before going back to full body armour. That is one experiment of laying down armour for them to build on.

Task 45

*What area of 'armour' might your character take off even if only for a short while?

(e.g. a behaviour or avoidance)

*What would it take for them to remove their armour?

*If you already have such a change in your story, have you given sufficient reason for it in the scene? What encouraged, pushed or forced them to try to drop their armour?

Your character may put full armour straight back on or they could leave that item off from that point.

Task 46

*If you are visually minded, you may wish to draw out a representation of your character with their armour in place at the start of the story and think about where they get to by the end.

Do they usually wear a helmet to not let certain comments in (such as not noticing a compliment), or wear a spiked full-body knights armour so nobody can get close to the real them underneath, or maybe they lift a shield up whenever the topic of settling down and having a baby comes up?

In some circumstances the experiment ends badly and the character may have an extra helmet and shield by the end! In others, only a breastplate remains over the heart or down by the side, ready to be put back on if a perceived threat increases.

Values

Your character may have been too busy chasing goals, doing what other people wanted or expected, or allowing anxiety to stop them doing what mattered to them. Or if you have a more negative arc, the character could get pulled away during the course of the story to focus or act in ways that are not in line with their values.

Task 47

*By the end of the story, is your character living more closely or further away from any of their highly rated values?

*If so, what is the impact on them?

(e.g. satisfaction, relationships, mood, or behaviour)

Perfectionism, Self-sabotage and Pleasers

You may find one of the changes in your character relates to them softening (or strengthening!) their tendency towards perfectionism, self-sabotage or being a people-pleaser. Again, it's important to consider change over time in increments including experiments with doing things differently. Even though a character may be able to see the downside to these ways of being, it's human nature to stick with what we know as change can feel threatening.

Task 48

*Does anything change across the story in terms of how perfectionism, self-sabotaging or people-pleasing tendencies show themselves or how much impact they have on the character?

*If so, what helps this change to happen?

Hidden longings, Hidden Feelings and Defence Mechanisms

We have looked at how healthy emotions and longings can be pushed away so hard and for so long that the character becomes unaware of them in their conscious mind. A key way in which internal change can take place in your character is that they start to become more aware of those hidden feelings and longings as their defence mechanisms fail or reduce.

If you want a realistic trajectory of hidden feelings or longings rising up into awareness, it is helpful to create multiple incidents across the storyline in which they rise up, get pushed away or deflected by a defence mechanism, but are that bit closer to the surface. Over several repetitions you can have a character who by the end of the story is able to feel their hidden emotion or longings.

Your character will be resistant to allowing their hidden aspects to hit them full in the face – remember that they are hidden for a reason! Their mind has 'disallowed' those emotions or longings based on past learning or avoidance of pain. This is why it's best to gently move your character across several scenes rather than one big 'revelation' where they suddenly understand and feel everything at once.

Imagine that hidden feelings or longings are stored in a cellar. That's the unconscious part of the mind the character doesn't have free access to. It's still part of the 'house' of their mind but it's locked away beneath the living space.

If something happens in a scene that triggers a hidden feeling or longing, it starts to escape out of the cellar, up the stone steps, towards the daylight in the garden. If the hidden feeling or longing makes it all the way up to the outdoors, your character gets a full dose of pain or attraction or grief or desire, or whatever has been forbidden. Your character doesn't want to feel this, it's too much! In jumps a defence mechanism to knock the hidden aspect down a few of those stone steps back towards the cellar. But this time, it may not be all the way buried in the dark. It may be on step two, that little bit closer to the sun shining a light on the truth.

Let's take an example of a character who has strict rules about not letting others down, that attending to her own needs is selfish, so she never says 'no' to people. How could she change across a story so that the healthy longing to be cared for by herself and others moves from cellar to garden?

Early in the story – she has moments of getting in touch with what she wants and a flicker of anger at being ordered around. She pushes that away immediately back towards the cellar.

By mid-story – she is starting to become aware of longings to care for herself, then becomes anxious and sabotages it, returning to the 'safety' of putting others first. But she starts to notice and plan self-care more and allows healthy anger to hang around for a few minutes when she's treated poorly. The longing hangs out on step five, halfway to daylight.

End of story – she has experimented with doing nice things for herself despite the discomfort of breaking her own 'rules'. She tries putting in some boundaries with others. The healthy longing is sitting on the porch in daylight so that she's aware but not confident and comfortable with it yet.

Of course this could have gone another way. She may have stuffed her longings back in the cellar and moved back in to care for her bullying parents! But at least the reader will have had the chance to understand and feel those longings on her behalf, making the ending feel more tragic.

Task 49

*Go back to one of the emotions or longings that you identified as being hidden to the character at the start of the story. Is it fully in the basement or on one of the ten steps towards the surface?

*Through your story, track or create moments where the hidden aspect gets triggered so that it moves up some steps into awareness, only to get booted back down with a defence mechanism.

You probably want a few of these moments in longer form writing so that the change isn't too fast and unrealistic.

*Where does the hidden feeling or longing get to by the end of the story? Pushed back down? Out in the sunlight? Somewhere in-between?

Who Knows What?

If you are interested in the unconscious aspects of your character such as hidden feelings or longings, it can be useful to map out who knows what and when.

You can then check:

- The way your character acts at certain points matches their insight at the time.
- That the trajectory of change isn't too fast to seem unlikely.
- How much mystery or insight you want for the reader and at what pace.

You can draw out a graph with your sections of story or chapters and mark it up for a particular longing or feeling. Show the following:

- The reader getting to know about the hidden elements.
- The character getting to know about them.

Keep it simple by only tracking one hidden element per diagram to start with.

In my example, the diagram tracks knowledge about a character's hidden longing for closeness (which initially appears as pushing others away).

Diagram 1: Mapping longing across the story for reader and character

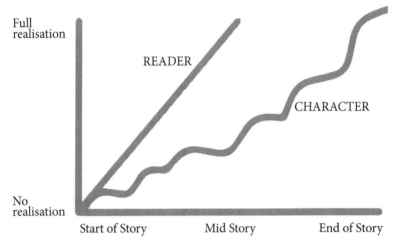

You will note your reader may work things out by your clues in a more linear fashion (in this case it is clear halfway through the story), building up a picture of the character as they read. However, the character is likely to have a wavy pattern as they push away insights using defence mechanisms to try to avoid painful or feared experiences as we looked at earlier with the idea of stairs going up from the basement.

In this example, each bump on the curve is a scene where the character's longing for closeness is triggered (e.g. someone being kind) which they momentarily are aware of, then push away (e.g. telling themselves that person is smothering then leaving the room). Over the course of the story, the character has more and more experiences of their hidden longing for closeness. The reader in this example has enough evidence by mid-story to realise what the character longs for. However, it takes until the end of the story for the character to gain this insight.

If you find this a useful method and you have a large pack of fancy pens at your disposal, you can add in when other key characters know about the hidden feeling or longing, or have more than one hidden element in the same diagram using another colour.

Character Summary

This book has covered many possible influencing factors when you consider your characters but don't let the information overwhelm you! Remember to place the learning in those deep pockets and only pull out what you need as you need it.

I suggest that for each main character you create a summary using the topics that most resonated or felt like a gap that was important to fill.

You may find it useful to draw up a list of the key questions to ask yourself (or another writer) about each main character.

When you have your summaries, you can also keep an eye out for too much overlap between characters. You may find that your own beliefs, longings and so on accidentally sneak in, creating a lack of clarity and difference between your characters. It can be those very differences that cause interesting clashes between them as well as opportunities for one character to learn from another, however begrudgingly.

Another training exercise is to take somebody else's story (such as by your favourite author) and see how much you've been able to read between the lines of the main character's internal world. Look back and see where the breadcrumbs were trailed so that you built up this rich picture and strong emotional response.

Then you can flick back to the beginning of Inside Fictional Minds and start all over again in depth with another of your own characters.

Further Reading

Attachment

There are numerous sources to find detail about the fascinating experiments and development of Attachment Theory by people like Bowlby and Ainsworth. Here you will learn in more detail about how attachment patterns show in childhood and in adult romantic relationships.

This site gives a great overview:

http://labs.psychology.illinois.edu/~rcfraley/attachment.htm

If you want to dive into more depth, this book is thorough but very readable. It crosses over into other topics we have touched on such as emotional regulation.

Attachment Across the Lifecourse: A brief introduction by David Howe (2011).

Coping

The coping strategies that I shared were taken from theoretical work in this area by Lazarus and Folkman in the 1980's. You can find a good summary of the coping strategies under

'Coping' on Wikipedia. There are coping questionnaires you can get online if you're interested in a breakdown of categories into example behaviours, such as the COPE inventory.

Defence mechanisms / Hidden longings and feelings

The idea of hidden feelings and longings that trigger defence mechanisms comes from Psychodynamic theory. Freud proposed the concept of defence mechanisms back in the nineteenth century. You may be interested in the various types of defence mechanisms by name (note that in the U.S. it is spelt 'defense mechanisms'). A great resource for thinking about them from the 'mature' to the more 'immature' end can be found here:

https://psychcentral.com/lib/15-common-defense-mechanisms

A relatable way to understand the purpose of defence mechanisms, how they appear, and what your character can do about them can be found in these self-help books which contain multiple examples of defences in action:

Why Did I Do That?: Psychological Defense Mechanisms and the Hidden Ways They Shape Our Lives by Joseph Burgo (2012).

The Lies We Tell Ourselves by Jon Frederickson (2017)

Narcissism

This is a useful summary article on Understanding the Mind of a Narcissist:

www.psychologytoday.com/us/blog/toxic-relationships/201804/understanding-the-mind-narcissist

This review article from Psychological Science is a more academic read if you want links to research. The full paper is free to read if you search for it online:

The 'Why' and 'How' of Narcissism: A Process Model of Narcissistic Status Pursuit by Grapsas, Brummelman and Back (2019).

There are many books written about the impact of being related to or in a relationship with a narcissist if you want to consider the impact on another character in the story.

Perception

I recommend that you take some time to look at the Cognitive Behaviour Therapy (CBT) model to understand more about what underlying view your character has about themselves, others and the world. This is one way to consider what 'glasses' your character wears as we looked at in the Perception chapter.

A good introduction for the model can be found in the book:

Cognitive Behavioural Therapy for Dummies by Branch and Wilson (2019).

You can read an accessible article here by the authors of this book, that focuses on core beliefs:

www.dummies.com/health/mental-health/core-beliefs-and-cognitive-behavioural-therapy/

Perfectionism

An article from the American Psychological Association gives more detail about perfectionism:

www.apa.org/monitor/nov03/manyfaces

The BBC has an article about the unhelpful aspects of perfectionism that includes some research evidence:

www.bbc.com/future/article/20180219-toxic-perfectionism-is-on-the-rise

Roles

The 'Parent Adult Child' model is used in Transactional Analysis which was developed by Eric Berne. Each of the three parts are called 'Ego States' which is the term to look up if you want to read more. There are some good summary videos on YouTube to explain this such as:

'Transactional Analysis 1: Ego States (Parent, Adult and Child Plus Subdivisions' by Lewis Psychology.

Rules

The 'rules' covered in this book are called 'Rules for Living' in the Cognitive-Behavioural Therapy (CBT) model. See the CBT book recommended under 'Perception'. The negative thinking patterns (sometimes called thinking traps) listed in this book also come from Cognitive Behaviour Therapy.

Self-sabotage

If you want to understand the experience of self-sabotage more and consider ways that your character may break these patterns, then a self-help book may be a good start. There are many available which cover different aspects of self-sabotage, such as:

The Healthy Mind Toolkit by Alice Boyes (2018).

She has written a summary article which you can access here:

https://greatergood.berkeley.edu/article/item/how_to_stop_sabotaging_yourself.

Teenagers

You can find resources on brain development by Professor Blakemore here including a TED talk and link to academic publications:

www.psychol.cam.ac.uk/staff/professor-sarah-jayne-blakemore

Her book is an accessible and in-depth look at the teenage brain:

Inventing Ourselves: The Secret Life of the Teenage Brain by Sarah-Jayne Blakemore (2019).

Trauma

The NHS website has a section on post-traumatic stress disorder if you want to read more or if you think the symptoms listed may apply to you and you want some help. MIND have useful information plus a route to support if you are in the UK.

www.nhs.uk/mental-health/conditions/post-traumatic-stress-disorder-ptsd

www.mind.org.uk - search 'trauma'

If your character has experienced a more significant level of trauma than we covered (such as abuse) you may find the following sources of evidence-based literature useful:

www.childtrauma.org

The Body Keeps the Score: Mind, Brain and Body in the Transformation of Trauma, Bessel van der Kolk (2015)

Values

The list of values to rate and the idea of using values as a guiding compass comes from Acceptance and Commitment Therapy (ACT). There are free resources for this model that could be useful, such as:

YouTube videos: See '*Values vs Goals by Dr Russ Harris*' and '*What are Values? From Your ACT Auntie*'

www.psychologytools.com/resource/values/

About the Author

Dr Stephanie Carty is a writer, NHS Consultant Clinical Psychologist and trainer with a qualification in teaching higher and professional education. Her fiction is widely published and has been shortlisted in competitions including the Bridport Prize, Bath Flash Fiction Award, Bristol Short Story Prize and Caterpillar Story for Children Prize. Her novella-in-flash *Three Sisters of Stone* won Best Novella in the Saboteur Awards. She is represented by Curtis Brown.

Author Acknowledgements

My thanks to everyone who has attended the face-to-face or online version of my course Psychology of Character for Writers. Your willingness to share, explore and question your characters helped me to create this workbook. A few of you suggested that I should write it!

I've been fortunate to have feedback, edit suggestions and general pompom waving from some fantastic members of the writing community. Huge thanks to Cat Lane, Louise Cobby, Judi Walsh and Debbi Voisey. Many more writers have been kind enough to reach out about their excitement for this book or have provided fantastic advanced praise for us to quote. A special mention to my wonderful writing friends Sophie van Llewyn and Hannah Persaud – you are both my fuel and my comfort blanket.

Thanks to my friend and writer Liz Kay who started the journey of bringing psychology to writers with me several years ago as part of the Writing Kiln.

The cover art for this book is more than I could have wished for from my talented friend and psychotherapist Louise Ryder. Thank you for capturing so beautifully the spirit of *Inside Fictional Minds*.

I'm so grateful to Jude Higgins and the Ad Hoc Fiction team for their interest in the possibilities of this book and helping it to exist outside of my head.

My final thank you is to you, the reader, for taking the time to open your mind to the ideas I've shared. I hope you explore any areas of interest to find out more from the amazing researchers and therapists who have increased our understanding of the most important questions for our characters: Why? What's underneath that? And what's underneath that?

Stephanie